Your copy of this book was proudly sponsored by:

_____

To learn more about this book and workshops, visit
www.tp-rewards.com/arewehomeyet

Are We Home Yet?

by Christie J. Jones, M.Ed.

Are We Home Yet?
Copyright (c) 2015 by Christie J. Jones
All rights reserved.

Published by TP Rewards
8647 Richmond Highway #659
Alexandria, VA 22309
www.tp-rewards.com

No Part of this publication may be reproduced, stored in a retrieval syste or transmitted in any way by any means, electronic, mechanical, photocopy, recording or otherwise withour written permission of the publisher except as provided by USA copyright law.

Book designed by TP Rewards, LLC
Illustrations by Eric Nyamor
Author photo by: Tierre S. Cobb, Anaya Photography

International Standard Book Number: 978-0-9860659-6-5
Library of Congress Control Number: 2014959449

Published in the United States of America

To learn more about this book and workshops, visit
www.tp-rewards.com/arewehomeyet

Hi, I'm Max. I'm in the 2nd grade and I like going to school!

I like my teacher and my friends.

Tomorrow a Leader

I wish I could live at school, because I don't like going home. I don't live in a house or an apartment. I live in a shelter.

Community Shelter

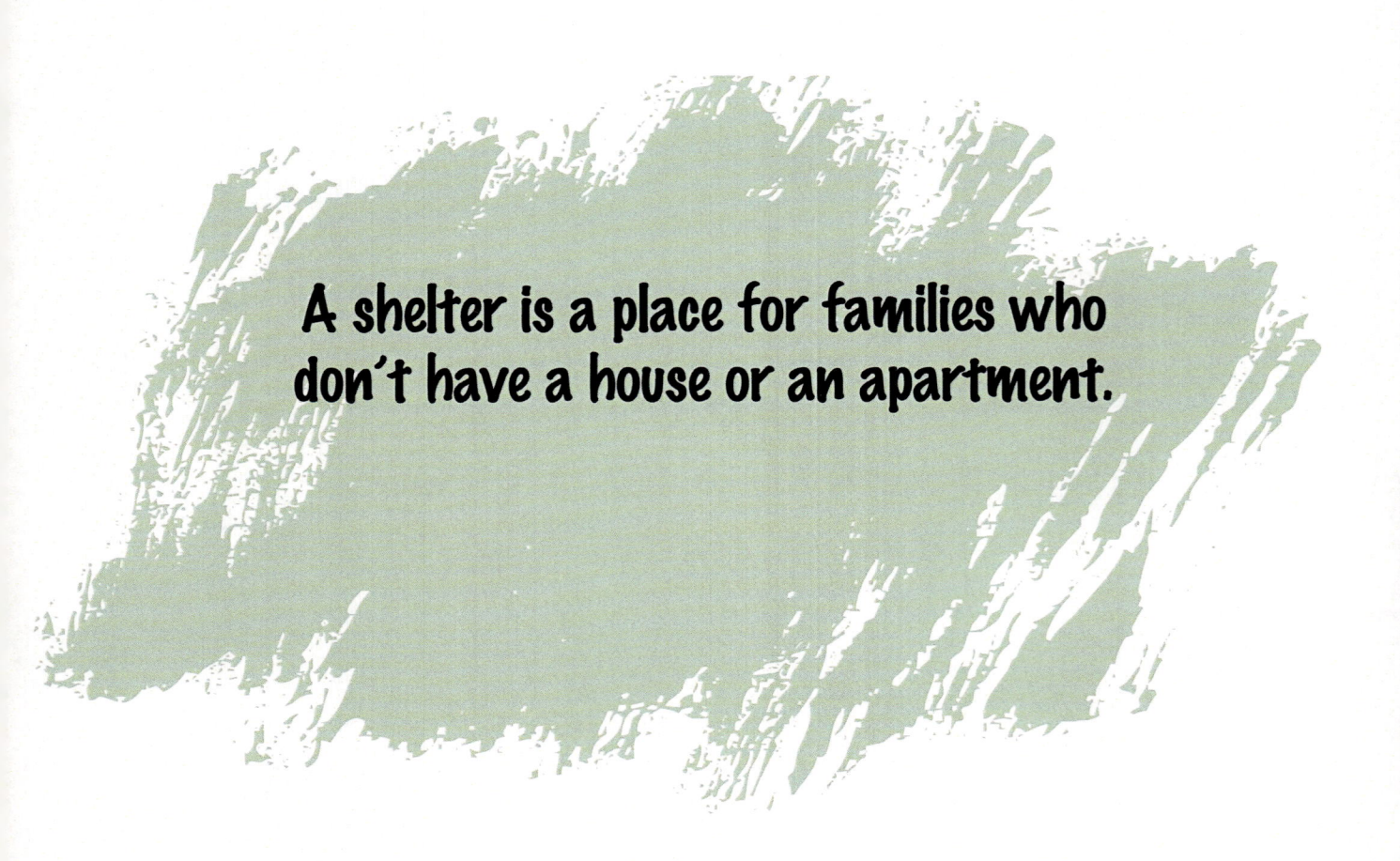

A shelter is a place for families who don't have a house or an apartment.

6

My family and I were forced to leave our apartment because my dad lost his job and we couldn't pay the bills.

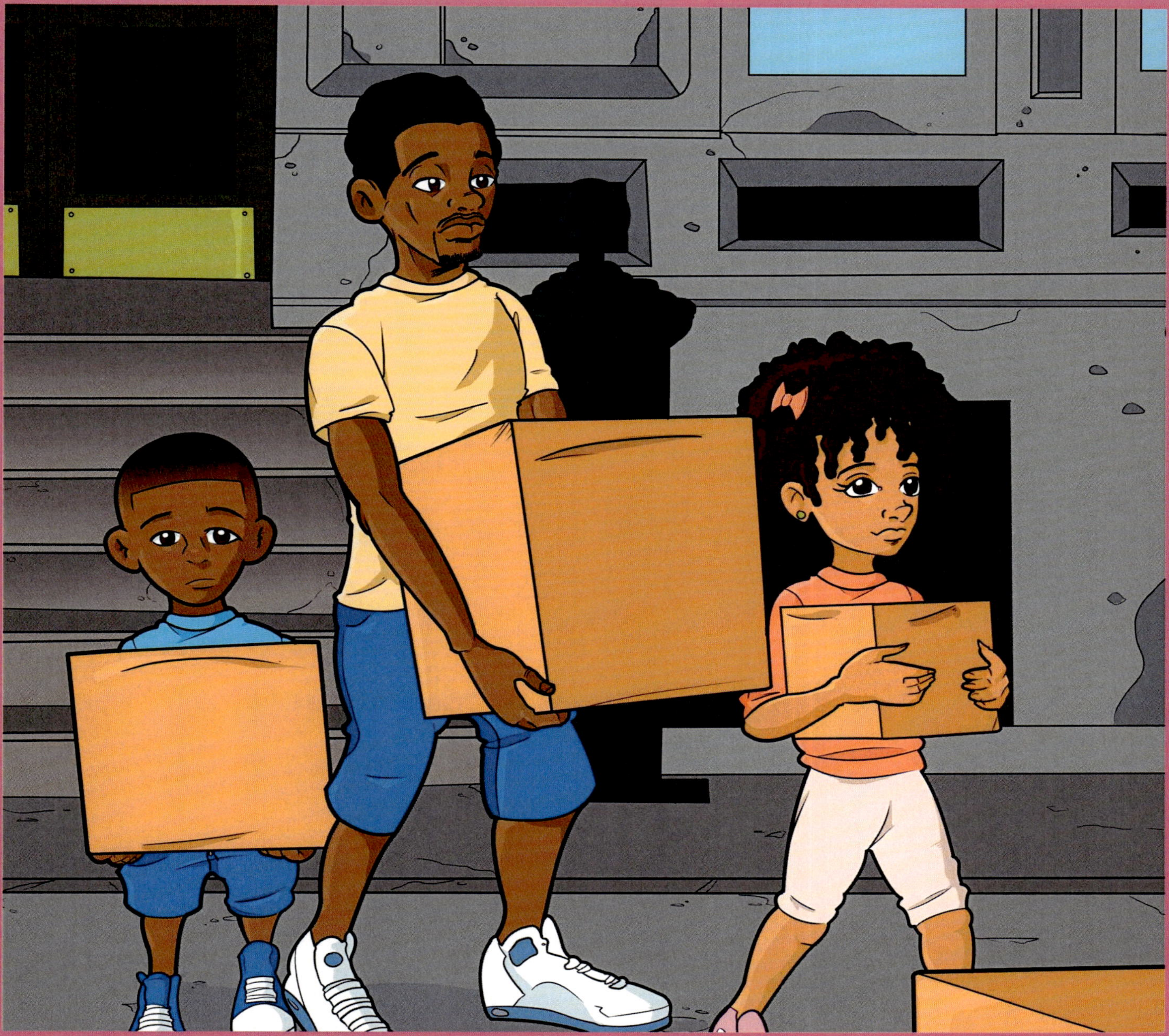

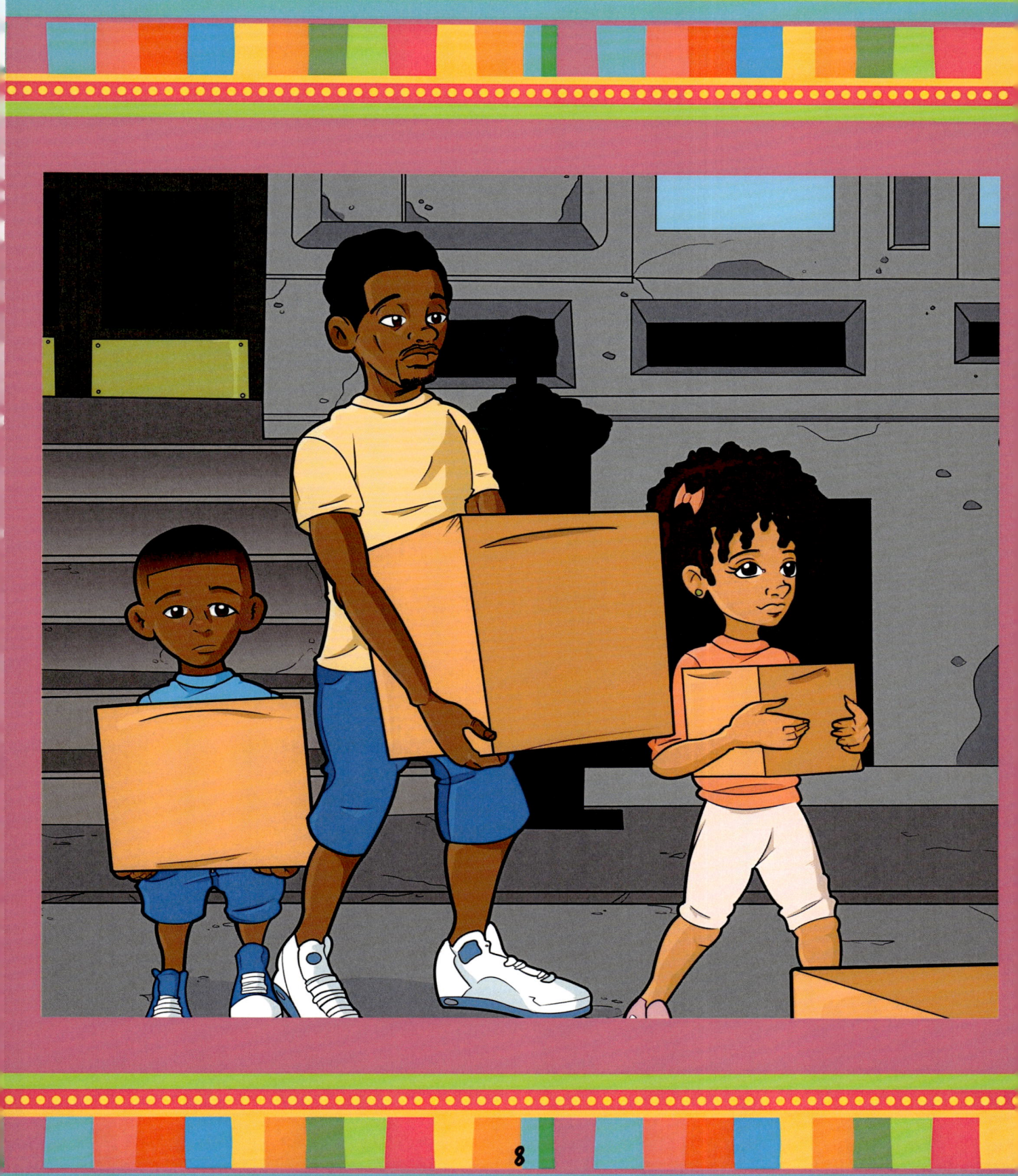

In the shelter, my sister and I stay in a room with our mom and another family.

The Smith family lives in the same room with us. Before coming to the shelter, they lived in their car.

The Roberts family lived in a motel before coming to the shelter.

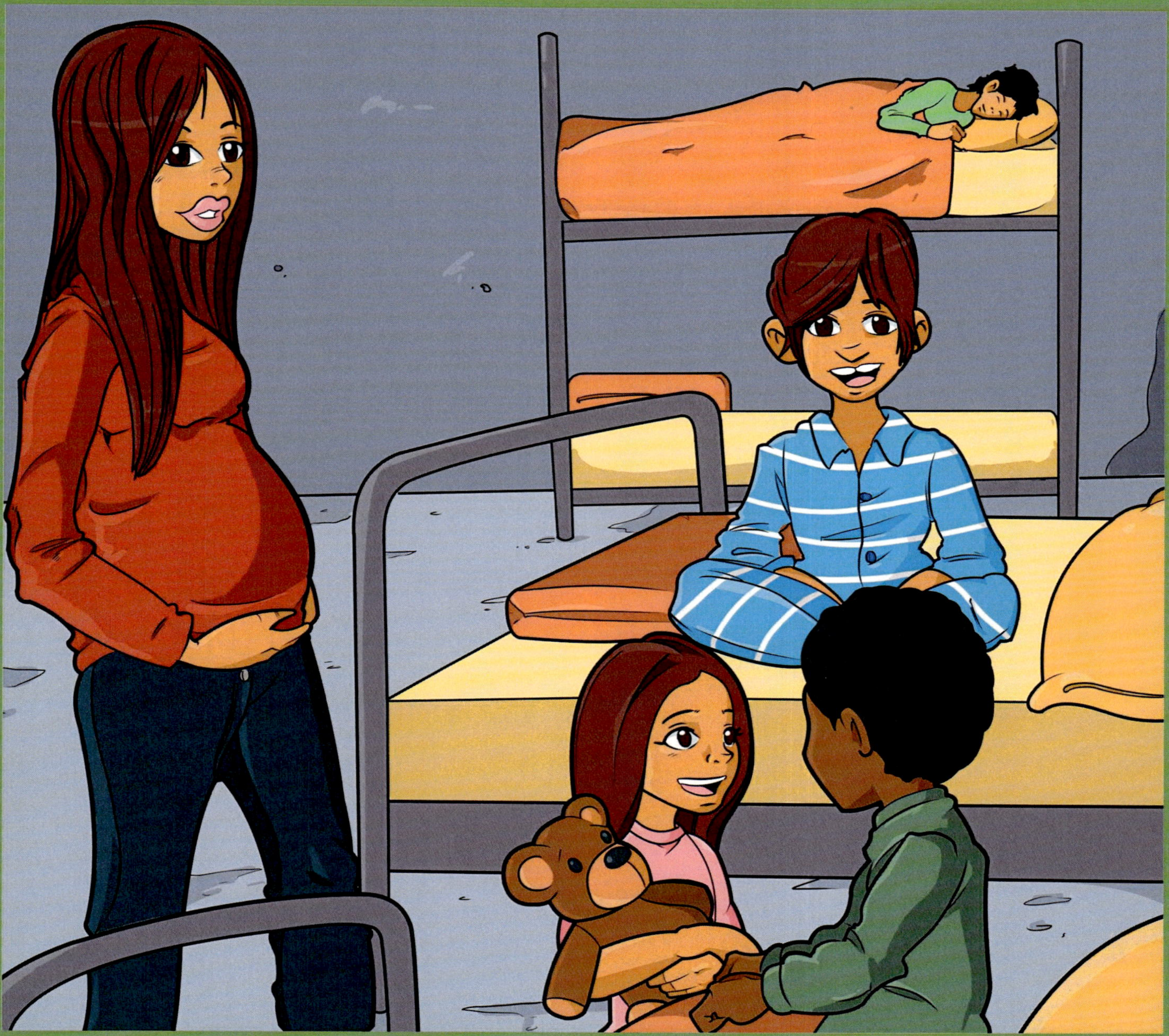

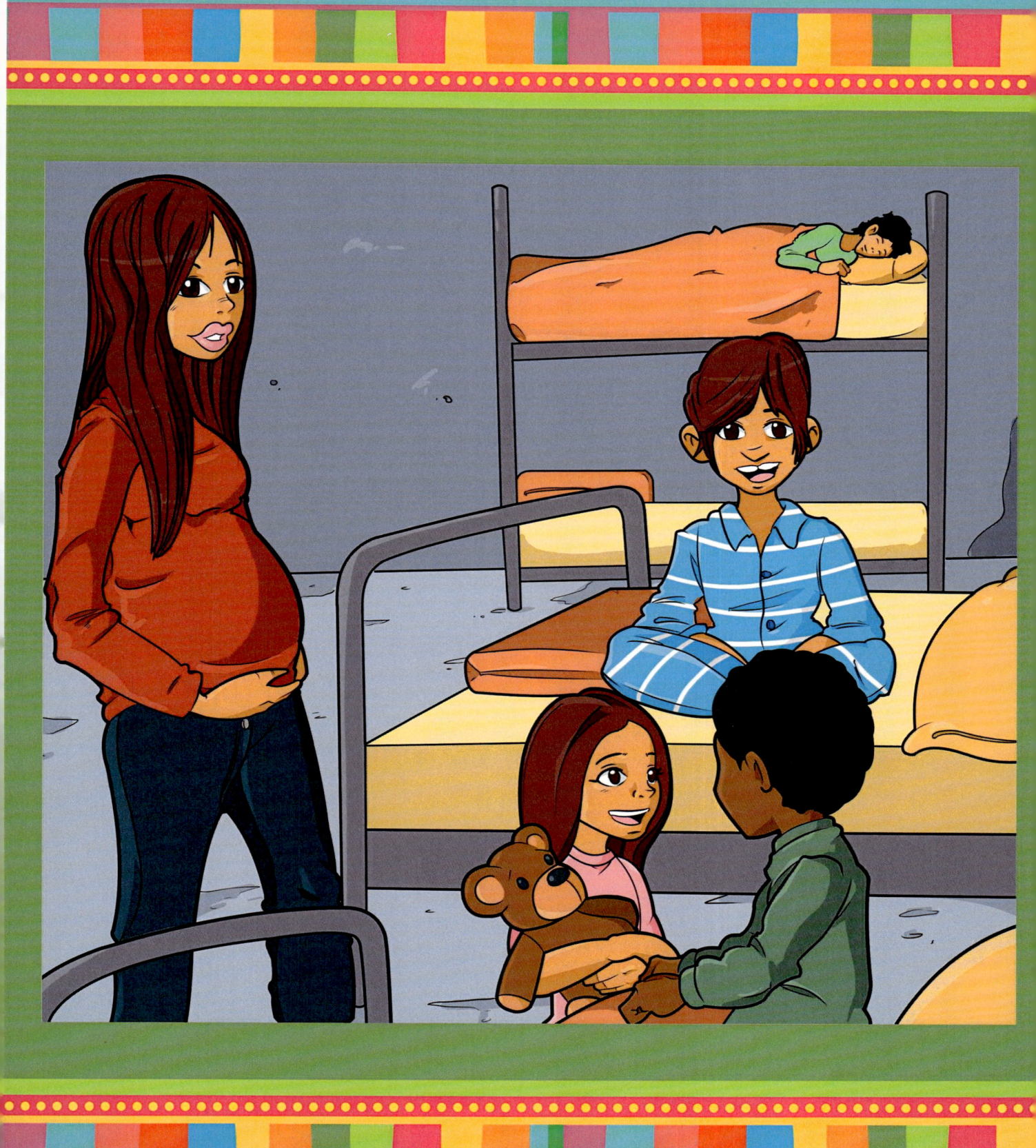

Sharing a room with other families makes me feel uncomfortable and afraid sometimes. I don't like being afraid, so I talk with people I trust about my feelings.

Mr. Mike is my adult friend at the shelter. He's nice. He helps me talk about my feelings and he teaches me how not to be angry or mad. When I'm angry, Mr. Mike tells me to read a book, or draw pictures, or talk to my parents, and pray.

12

Sometimes I get angry when I see my classmates riding to school in their cars, while I have to ride to school on a special van. At other times, I get angry when my classmates have new clothes or toys my family can't buy.

Mr. Mike and I talked about the things that I want and the things that I need. I want new clothes and toys but my family needs a home to live in. And we all need food, clothes and water to live. My talks with him helps me stay calm.

14

I get embarrassed when kids pick on me for not having cool toys. I sometimes worry that kids at my school won't be my friend when they find out I live at the shelter.

However, Mr. Mike says good friends are kind to everyone, no matter where they live.

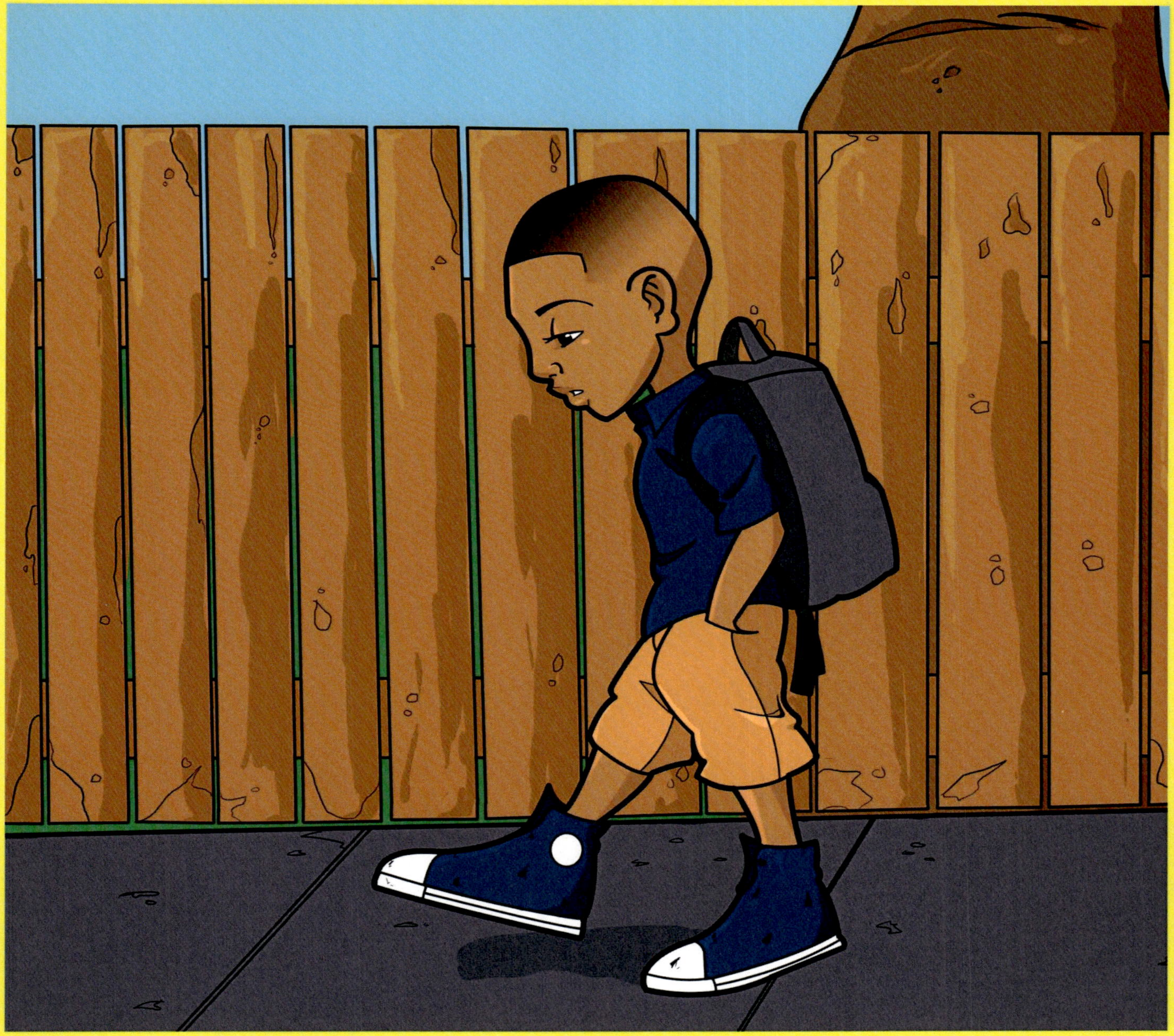

We learned about teasing in school. If someone is using words to hurt you, you need to talk to an adult you trust. I'm glad I have a teacher, and a school counselor I can talk to at school.

We drew pictures of what it means to treat others the way you want to be treated. I drew a picture of me sharing my crayons with my classmates.

Treat others the way you want to be treated.

That's why I like school! It is the only place I have my own desk with my supplies and my space!

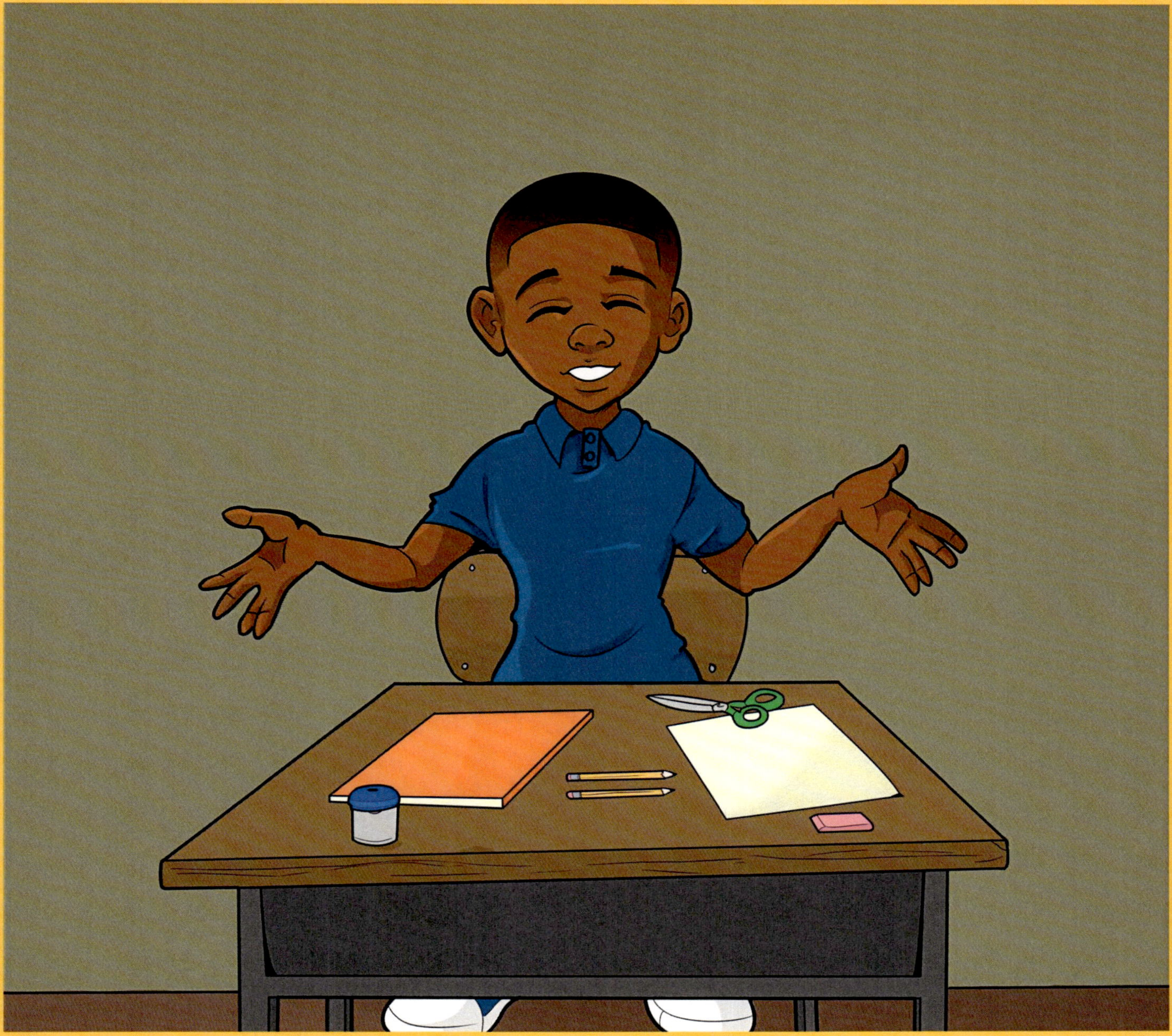

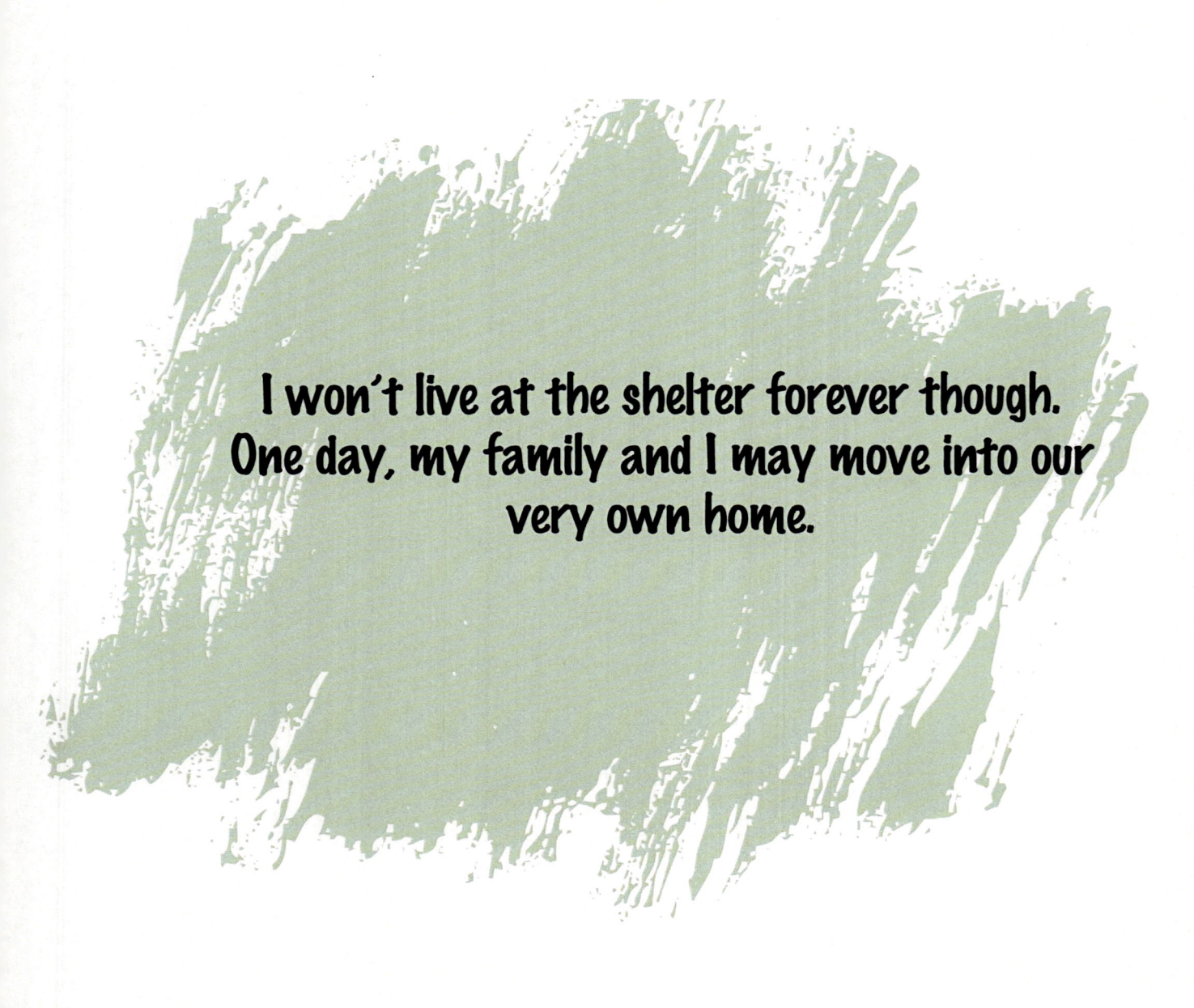

I won't live at the shelter forever though. One day, my family and I may move into our very own home.

22

To learn more about this book and workshops, visit
www.tp-rewards.com/arewehomeyet

Made in the USA
Middletown, DE
26 February 2015